Macramé

In easy steps

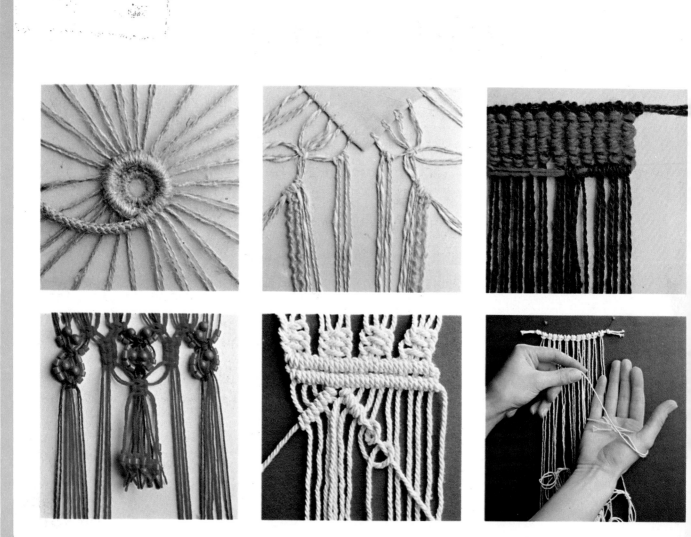

Macramé
In easy steps

Barbara Pegg

Studio Vista
London

Written by Barbara Pegg
Photographs by Alan Don

A Studio Vista book published by
Cassell & Collier MacMillan Publishers Ltd.,
35 Red Lion Square, London WC1R 4SG
and at Sydney, Auckland, Toronto, Johannesburg,
an affiliate of
Macmillan Publishing Co. Inc.,
New York.

Copyright © Studio Vista 1977
First published in 1977

ISBN 0 289 70789 7

Photoset by Amos Typesetters, Hockley, Essex

Printed by Sackville Press Billericay Limited, Billericay, Essex

Contents

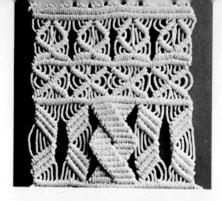

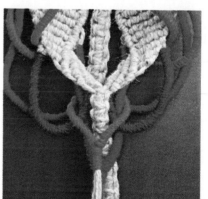

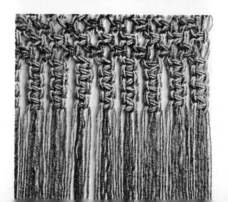

Introduction to Macramé

Illustrated on the left is a selection of materials and equipment necessary for the projects in this book.

Starting at top left, you will see a piece of softboard and pins for mounting (we used glassheaded pins as they are more readily visible); a selection of coloured yarns (wool, string and cotton of various weights); a cushion which could be used for mounting instead of a board; a selection of glass and wooden beads of various sizes; a tape measure, flat stick, piece of round wooden dowel rod, scissors, glue and a crochet hook.

Most of what you will need can be found in your local haberdashery, handicraft shop or department store, and on page 64 you will find a list of specialist suppliers.

Tying knots is such a simple everyday activity that we rarely give it much thought. In its various forms, it goes back so far, and into so many cultures, that it is impossible to know its origins. Since primitive man learnt to interlock one or more elements into some kind of structure, knotting has developed as a functional part of daily life and then, later, as a decorative feature. We can safely assume that it is one of the earliest craft forms, closely associated with weaving in its uses.

Macramé is a word which has been adopted as a comprehensive name for the different kinds of knots we know today, although the word has only been used since the nineteenth century. Its origins are obscure, but the two most likely possibilities are from the Turkish word *makrama,* meaning a scarf or napkin with a fringe, or the Arabic word *migramah,* a veil. Historically, macramé can be traced back to the Middle East in the ninth century B.C., and illustrations still survive of warriors wearing tunics edged with knotted fringes. After the Crusades, macramé came to Italy, where by the fifteenth century it became closely associated with bobbin and needlepoint lace, and was inset into cloth or used again as fringes. In the sixteenth century macramé borders were used extensively on ecclesiastical vestments. By the eighteenth century it was a popular craft in northern Europe, and came into its own in England in the Victorian era, with the fashion for extremely ornate furnishings. Macramé has also been closely associated with sailors' knots, particularly in the nineteenth century, and many of the fancy knots we know today were derived from them.

This book is designed to teach you a selection of knots, and it offers a wide choice of projects in which you can use the knots in different ways to achieve very varied results. The first project of a sampler is important in that it gives you a good basic knowledge of knots and it is well worth making this before attempting the other projects.

Macramé is a relatively simple craft to take up, because it requires very little equipment. All you need is a piece of softboard, pins, a selection of yarns or strings and a tape measure, and you are ready to begin.

Sampler One

1 The lark's head knot is used to mount threads. 20 threads of string will give you 40 single threads.

2 The square knot as braids, step one. The threads are worked in groups of four.

You will need:
300g (¾lb) of cotton string
Piece of dowel 12 × 225mm
(½ × 9in)
Softboard 450 × 300mm
(18 × 12in)
Glass-headed pins
Elastic bands
Tape measure
Scissors

Length of threads:
20 threads 8m (8yd) long

One of the best ways to begin learning macramé is by making a sampler. In the past, in many of the applied crafts a sampler was a fairly small piece of work carried out in order to discover techniques and design. On completion, it became not only a point of reference for further work, but also a decorative item in its own right.

In the same way, this first macramé sampler will enable you to learn the basic knots you will need in the early projects of the book, added to which you will have a very attractive wallhanging to enjoy looking at. To the beginner, macramé is deceptive. It looks intricate and difficult to do, but in actual fact it is surprisingly simple.

Most of the projects in this book consist of only one or two basic knots, tied in different patterns.

Preparation
For most of the pieces of macramé you will do, a piece of softboard and glass-headed pins are invaluable. Alternatively you could use a firm, flat cushion. This working surface will enable you to tie knots neatly and firmly, and pinning the threads and knotted areas down every so often will also help you shape the patterns.

The first thing you do is measure the length of the threads required. Throughout the book, the word 'threads' will be used to refer to the lengths of cotton, wool, string, etc. that you are using. Those threads which are placed across others, and are then knotted over, are referred to as leaders.

A simple rule-of-thumb guide to help you judge the length of the threads is to decide the finished size of your work, and then to measure each thread seven to eight times that size. As you can see (1) each single thread will give you two working threads when it is mounted on the piece of dowel in the position known as the lark's head. You may find it helpful to find two things such as chairs or door handles the required distance apart, round which you can wind all the threads continuously. Cut them at one end only, and the middle of each thread will then be your loop for mounting.

After you have mounted all the threads and before you begin to tie your first knots, you will need to wind each thread in a figure of eight motion from the end, about 300mm (12in) in length (see 1, page 14). This is to stop the individual threads from getting tangled while you are working.

The knots

The horizontal clove hitch knot (8) should be tied evenly and firmly. It may help if, when you have made the first loop around the leader, you hold this tightly with your thumb and forefinger, and pull the second loop up to it. You can pin the leader down at the side of your board to ensure it stays at the right angle. Note how the hitch loops to right or left, depending on which side your leader is. A complete row of hitches across the sampler makes a neat division between each pattern.

In the second part of the sampler, you will be learning how to tie the vertical clove hitch (see 22, page 11). This knot begins by taking a single thread, which formerly was used as leader, and looping it around each thread in turn. Again, like the horizontal clove hitch, this thread can loop to right or left depending on which side you are working towards. The combination of these two hitches, when worked in colour, can be a simple way of creating striking patterns and shapes. The alternating chains (see 27, page 12) are quick to do and effective as braids.

3 The square knot, step two. Make 10 braids with five square knots to each braid.

4 The square knot as alternating pattern, row one. Leave two threads at the end of each row.

5 Row two, tie all threads. Make five rows in all, alternating rows one and two.

6 The half-knot. Working in groups of four, tie only step one of the square knot.

7 After the fifth knot, turn the outer two threads around. Make 10 braids of 15 half knots each.

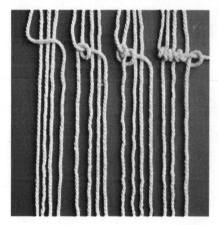

8 The horizontal clove hitch. The left thread is the leader. Each thread loops around it twice.

9

9 Make two rows of horizontal hitches below the half-knot braids to complete the first section.

10 The sampler is already beginning to look quite decorative, using three variations of one basic knot.

11 The clove hitch diamond pattern. Work in groups of 10, placing the leaders diagonally.

12 The lower half of the diamond pattern. Cross the leaders over, using pins to hold them in place.

13 Tie a row of hitches below each diamond and a complete row from right to left.

14 The clove hitch cross pattern. Work in groups of 10 and cross the leaders over in the centre.

15 The completed cross pattern. Make a row of horizontal hitches from left to right.

16 The clove hitch chevron pattern. Work in two groups of 14 threads each side of the sampler.

17 Completing the clove hitch chevron pattern. Keep the three rows of hitches close together.

18 The clove hitch interlocking pattern. Use six of the centre 12 threads to begin and tie seven rows.

19 Repeat in opposite direction with the remaining six threads, so that this group overlaps the first.

20 Tie seven more rows with each group to complete. Make a row of hitches across the sampler.

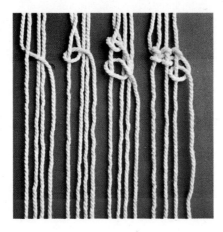

21 By this stage, the sampler is half complete. This section is composed entirely of clove hitches.

22 The vertical clove hitch. The left thread is looped twice round each thread in turn.

23 With 10 threads on the right of the sampler, tie four rows from left to right.

24 One row of horizontal and four of vertical hitches right to left. Repeat this pattern on the left side.

25 Working first with 10 of the centre threads, tie one row of vertical hitches left to right.

26 Tie six rows of horizontal hitches with a vertical hitch at each end of every row.

27 Alternating chains with two and four threads. The right thread loops round the left, and vice versa.

28 Alternating chains looping twice with each thread. Shown here with two and four threads.

29 Working across the sampler, put a bead on alternate pairs of threads, with three chains in between.

30 The main design of the sampler is completed and you are now familiar with the basic knots of macramé.

31 Use 12 threads each side of the sampler. Three beads and chains are tied together with two square knots.

32 The centre 16 threads are tied in four square knot braids with a bead between each knot.

Beads

Using beads adds an extra decorative quality to macramé. Take care when you are looking for beads to choose those with holes the right size for the thread. In this sampler, two threads have been put through one bead. If you prefer, you can slip your bead onto only one of the two threads. It may help when you are threading the beads to thin the ends of the thread a little, and then dab on a touch of glue. When the thread is dry, the beads will slip on easily.

Finishing

The finishing touches are made to the sampler by putting beads on all the strings, securing each bead with an overhand knot. Finally, fray the ends of thread to create an additional decorative effect.

Mounting

Mount two threads at either end of the piece of dowel, and tie alternating chains. Join the two chains with a tight square knot, and fray these ends too.

Looking back at all the steps of the sampler, you can now see that it is only made up of three basic knots. These are the square knot, one part of it, the half-knot, two different kinds of clove hitch knots and the alternating chain.

With this basic vocabulary of knots, you are now able to carry out all the projects in the first half of this book. One of the most attractive features of macramé is that you can work in many threads and yarns to achieve widely different results, while still using only a few knots. Some of the most striking and beautiful pieces of macramé are simple repetitions of one or two basic knots, allowing the colour or texture of the thread to accentuate the design of the finished work.

33 Tie four square knots and five rows of horizontal hitches either side of the centre in a fan shape.

34 Take in two threads to the centre group with each square knot, until all the threads are tied together.

35 The sampler is completed by binding the five groups tightly and threading beads on the ends.

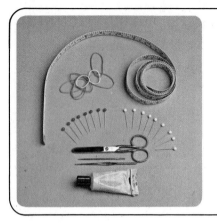

Mounting and Finishing

This section is all about various ways of beginning and ending macramé, which you will need to know for most of the projects throughout the book.

The threads you need for tying macramé knots have to be up to seven or eight times the actual finished length. This varies according to the type and density of the knots used, but if you are beginning a piece of work where you have decided the length you want and are not certain exactly which knots you want to use, it is better to be on the safe side and cut to the maximum length, rather than run out three-quarters of the way down.

If you are working on a piece which is going to measure less than 150 × 100mm (6 × 4in) when finished, you can probably leave your threads hanging down from the board without any danger of them becoming tangled. For anything longer and wider you will need to wind your threads into individual bundles so that they are easy to control, and so that you can take them in turn as required. The simplest way of doing this is shown in steps 1 and 2 where you take each end of a thread and wind it up in a figure of

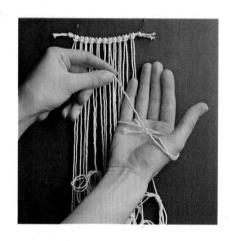

1 Starting from the end, wind the threads in a figure of eight around the thumb and little finger.

2 Secure the threads in a figure of eight, or butterfly, with an elastic band in the middle.

3 A group of threads mounted on thread bearers, pinned down and ready to begin.

4 Mounting the lark's head sideways, to begin tying knots or to add new threads.

eight, or butterfly, and then secure it in the middle with an elastic band. Wind each thread up to about 300mm (12in) from the top. As you use up the thread in knotting, pull each bundle out a little further. If your threads are too long or thick to wind around your hand, you could use the legs of a chair or something else which is the right distance apart.

Another way of tying up the ends of threads is to wind them onto bobbins or strips of card. If you cut a little nick in the edge of the card, you can catch the thread in it to prevent it slipping.

Mounting

Step 3 shows a typical way of setting up macramé, by mounting the threads onto thread bearers using the lark's head knot.

This knot can be worked from either side. As you can see, from each mounted lark's head you gain two working threads. In quite a few of the projects in this book, these threads are taken and tied in pairs. This is because some fine single threads tend to tie into very small and tight knots. Pairs of threads used together give extra body to the knots.

Another point to remember when mounting with the lark's head is to keep the threads fairly close together. Spacing them out to the width you want will only mean that as soon as you start tying the threads, the knots will pull them together again. The lark's head can be mounted sideways as well (4). When tying an area of vertical clove hitches, a thread mounted like this can be used as the leader, instead of the first of your threads on the right or left side. As leaders tend to get used up more quickly than other threads, this is a great help. Equally, you can add a new thread in this way when one runs out, mounting onto the next thread across. The short end can be hooked or darned into the back. The lark's head is also a simple way of introducing another colour when you are trying vertical clove hitches.

Another way to mount macramé is to start with all the threads laid flat on the board, and another one placed across them as a leader. Each thread is then tied round the leader with a horizontal clove hitch (5).

Finishing

The last method of mounting threads is also a very useful way of finishing when you want a straight edge to end with, which will correspond with a beginning mounted with lark's heads.

Steps 6, 7 and 8 show ways of finishing threads. For ends which are to hang free, added weight in the form of wrapping or beards helps the threads to fall more neatly and evenly.

If the macramé needs an edge of knots, with no threads visible at all, the ends can be darned into the back, either by pulling them through with a crochet hook (8), or by using a blunt tapestry needle with a large eye.

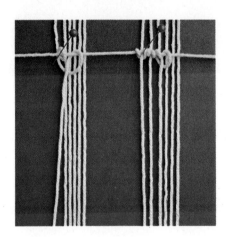

5 Another way to begin is to lay a leader across all the threads and tie a row of horizontal clove hitches.

6 Finishing the ends of the threads by wrapping them in groups, using a tapestry needle.

7 Finishing the ends of thread by tying overhand knots and threading on beads.

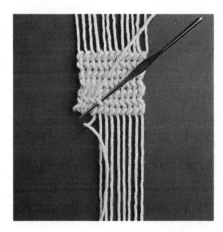

8 Finish by darning the ends into the back of the knots, pulling them through with a crochet hook. Trim.

Belt

You will need:
50g (2oz) mustard wool
50g (2oz) dark brown wool
150g (6oz) rust wool
Softboard and pins
Crochet hook
Darning needle

Length of threads:
For each half of the belt:
4 mustard threads 4m
(4yd) long
8 dark brown threads 4m
(4yd) long
20 rust threads 4m
(4yd) long
2 rust threads 100mm (4in)

long for mounting
7 rust threads 150mm (6in)
long for each tassel

Colour sequence:
R = rust
M = mustard
B = dark brown
RMBRBRRBRBMR

Here is a simple project which serves as a good introduction to macramé because it is a simple pattern worked to a narrow measure and can therefore be completed fairly quickly. The use of different coloured threads

brings an even richer effect to the pattern of the knots. In this case, the colours used are tonally related, but you may like to experiment with contrasting colours which would create an entirely different effect.

First mount your threads in the order indicated above. As this belt is made in knitting wool, which has a soft springy quality, it is better to work the threads in pairs. Knots in single wool usually tend to pull very tight, and are not always even. Because of this, remember to wind the ends in pairs to the right working length.

1 The first half of the pattern is two diagonal rows of hitches from the centre.

2 Tie four square knots in the centre. Complete the diamond pattern. Loop alternating chains at the sides.

3 Repeat the whole pattern four times. Tie four rows of diagonal hitches.

The pattern is made up of a main centre area of diamond shapes, with alternating chains either side which slot through the sides of each diamond. They should form a slight curve between each diamond.

The belt is made in two pieces which are then joined at the centre back, and it is worn tied at the front. Make the join by hemming each piece together with a needle and rust wool. Ends of wool are also darned in with a needle.

To finish the belt you will need to use a crochet hook to pull the threads back to the wrong side (4). The remaining four rust threads at each end are tied in alternating chains. To join the tassels, slip the seven threads halfway through the last loop of the chain, and with the wool from the chain bind the top of each tassel. Tie a tight knot and trim off the ends.

Variations

You could, of course, try making another belt made in one piece. If it is to be tied at the front, the threads at the end can be made into braids, and then extra lengths of wool added to the end you started from, to be knotted into matching braids.

Alternatively, threads can be mounted straight onto the bar of a buckle. Finish by darning the ends back so that the belt has a neat edge which can be pulled through the buckle easily.

Try using different types of material for making belts. A fine rayon or cotton thread with braids will be delicate, and a smooth-textured string belt mounted on a wood buckle will be chunky and casual.

You could also make handles for bags or a simple choker in the same way.

4 Darn the ends in at the back, all except the four chain threads, two of which are pulled to the front.

5 Make alternating chains 150mm (6in) long and join tassels to the ends of the threads.

Choker

You will need:
Two 25g (2oz) balls crochet
cotton, pale blue and turquoise
18 round deep blue beads
14 square turquoise beads
Softboard and pins
Crochet hook, tape measure
Transparent glue

Length of threads:
2 pale blue threads 1.5m (1½yd)
2 turquoise threads 1.5m (1½yd)
as leaders
12 pale blue threads 2m (2yd)
12 turquoise threads 2m (2yd)

Colour sequence:
B = pale blue
T = turquoise
BBBTTTTTTBBB

In this project the beginning is
different as the threads are not
mounted. Instead lay the threads
flat on your board in the right
order, and find the centre. You
can mark a line on the board as a
guide. The first leader lies along
this line, over the threads, and
knotting begins here. Work the
knots to one end, then turn the
board round and follow the steps
to the other end. The knots are
tied with double threads.

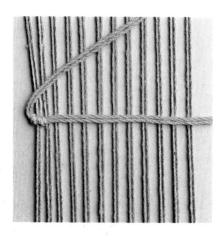

1 Place the turquoise leader across
the middle of the threads, with its
centre at the left side.

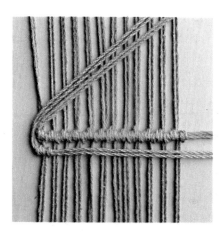

2 One row of horizontal hitches is
followed by another, with the pale
blue thread as leader.

3 Thread on beads as shown,
graduating the number of beads to
create a radiating pattern.

4 Tie two rows of hitches diagonally
below the beads. On the right, tie six,
then four, alternating chains.

5 Repeat steps 2 to 4 one more time, so that your choker will now look like this.

6 Tie three rows of horizontal hitches, then tie six alternating chains with each pair of threads.

7 Make five alternating chains with the centre threads, and three either side.

8 Tie four diagonal rows of hitches towards the middle and make a centre braid of 24 chains.

9 Hook the ends through on the wrong side, trim and secure with glue. Thread two beads on the chain. Tie.

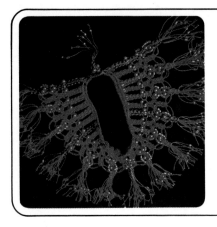

Necklet

You will need:
50g (2oz) shiny crochet cotton in scarlet
25g (1oz) in cerise pink
25g (1oz) in purple
460 small scarlet beads
84 round cerise pink beads
Softboard and pins
Transparent glue

Length of threads:
6 purple threads 1m (1yd) long as thread bearers
62 scarlet threads 1.5m (1½yd) long
14 purple threads 1.5m (1½yd) long
24 cerise pink threads 1.5m (1½yd) long

Colour sequence:
P = purple
S = scarlet
C = cerise pink
(read colours from left to centre, then back again for right half of necklet)
PSSP SCCS CSSC SSSS
CSSC SSSS
PCCP SSSS CSSC SPPS
CSSC SSSS
PS centre

The necklet shown here, with its use of rich colours and tiny beads,

1 Mount the threads on four thread bearers. Tie a row of hitches over the other two bearers.

2 Working in groups of eight, put two scarlet beads on the centre threads. Tie four square knots.

3 Put on pink and scarlet beads, twisting the outer threads in each group. Tie two square knots.

4 Tie one square knot between each group. Thread on more pink and scarlet beads as shown.

has a rich ornamental quality reminiscent of Egyptian jewelry from the time of the Pharaohs.

It could be made as a collar to be attached to a dress or blouse, and would add distinction to a plain dress, especially if worked in gold or silver, with gold or silver or crystal beads, as in the jewelry project (page 30). Hem the collar to the neck edge of the dress or blouse with matching or invisible thread.

To make the necklet, the threads are mounted on four thread bearers and knotted down from the top in pairs. The ends of the thread bearers form the fastening. Pin the threads down to the board often, to keep the knots in their correct positions. Make the spaces between each group slightly wider as you work down the pattern, so that the necklet forms a curve.

The type of thread recommended here is shiny crochet cotton. It is advisable to use cotton, even matt if you cannot get the shiny kind. A rayon or nylon thread is often difficult to tie knots with, for although it may be shiny it will also be very slippery to work with on such a small scale.

5 Tie one square knot below the beads. Put on more beads. Tie three square knots with scarlet threads.

6 Finish each group with two square knots. Add scarlet beads. Trim to 50mm (2in).

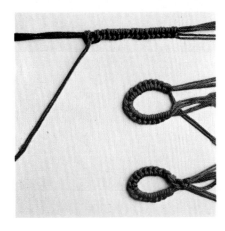

7 Make a loop on the left side of the necklet with the purple bearers, 50mm (2in) long.

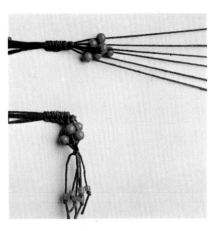

8 Make a group of beads and tassels on the right. Trim the ends and secure with glue.

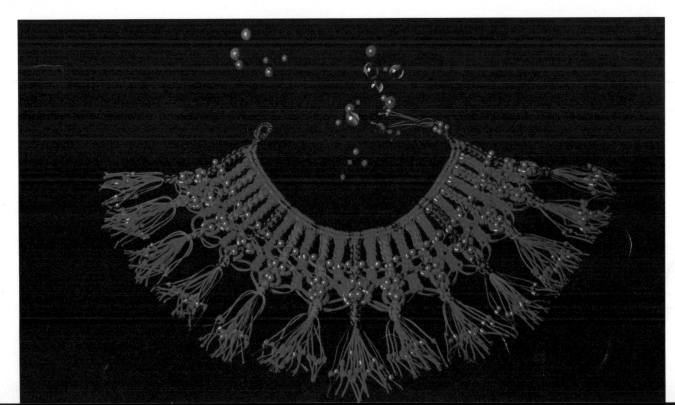

Shawl

You will need:

For the fringe:
200g (8oz) lemon yellow linen yarn
100g (4oz) deep yellow bouclé wool
Fine crochet hook

For the shawl:
Triangle of yellow fabric 2m (2yd) wide × 1m (1yd) deep
Yellow cotton

Length of threads:
184 yellow linen threads 1.75m (1¾ yd) long for sides
8 yellow linen threads 1.75m (1¾ yd) long for point
44 yellow bouclé threads 1m (1yd) long for sides
2 yellow bouclé threads 1m (1yd) long for point
1 yellow bouclé thread 3.5m (3½ yd) long for two edges

One of the most attractive ways of using macramé is for fringes. The shawl on these pages has a lacy fringe made up of square knots, half knots and alternating chains.

The yarn used here is a mixture of cotton and linen, spun with a twist, and bouclé wool. You could use cotton or rayon thread or alternatively slightly thicker wool, which would suit a lightweight woollen fabric for the shawl itself. Another idea would be to put small beads on the ends of the threads, to make an especially decorative shawl. They would also weight the fringe a little and make it hang better.

The shawl itself is quite a large one, and to cut a triangle this size you will need fabric which is 1.5m (1½ yd) wide and 1.5m (1½ yd) in length. Fold the square of fabric in half diagonally and cut. Machine or hand hem the edges.

Hook the linen threads through

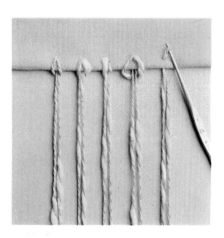

1 Machine the edges of the fabric and hook linen threads into the two sides of the shawl.

2 Tie two rows of single alternating square knots, spacing them fairly loosely.

3 Tie a row of half knot braids, making 12 knots in each braid. Position them exactly between the square knots.

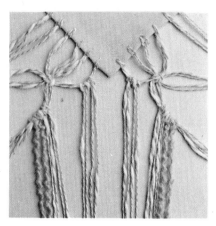

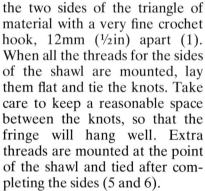

4 Mount bouclé threads with the lark's head, as shown and tie seven alternating chains.

5 The point of the shawl. Mount more linen and bouclé threads with lark's head knots.

6 Tie a square knot at the centre, with half knot braids and alternating chains either side.

the two sides of the triangle of material with a very fine crochet hook, 12mm (½in) apart (1). When all the threads for the sides of the shawl are mounted, lay them flat and tie the knots. Take care to keep a reasonable space between the knots, so that the fringe will hang well. Extra threads are mounted at the point of the shawl and tied after completing the sides (5 and 6).

When you have completed the fringe, lay the yellow bouclé along the two edges, and catch it down with a needle and cotton.

If you are able to knit or crochet, you may want to make your own shawl and knot a macramé fringe with the same wool to give it an individual touch.

Variations
As already mentioned in the introduction, it is probable that the word macramé originally meant a fringe. Try looking at some books on early knots and macramé, particularly the *Encyclopedia of Needlework* by Thérèse de Dillmont or *The Ashley Book of Knots* by Clifford Ashley, listed in the bibliography at the back of this book, to give you some ideas.

A wide variety of fringes and decorative edgings were made in the Victorian era in England, as decoration for tablecloths and soft furnishings, as well as for fashion accessories such as shawls, scarves and bags. They were sometimes mounted straight onto an existing piece of fabric, as the shawl in this project, or made as a separate edging to be sewn on when the knots were completed. This method is very like the type of furnishing braids which can be bought complete by the length in upholstery shops now, except they are, of course, machine-made and often not so delicate.

You might want to take some of the patterns from Victorian fringes (you could copy some from examples in books and museums), and adapt them to your own ideas. A soft and shiny type of rayon thread is available in haberdashery stores which is particularly suitable for furnishing fringes.

If you mount your fringe onto a piece of furnishing fabric, such as velvet or heavy linen, you could decorate the edges above the fringe with the type of braid illustrated in the project on applied macramé (page 50). This would give added depth and richness to the edging. As the fringe is the main feature, the braids could simply be appliquéd in straight lines along the edge or alternatively several rows could make a formal pattern, repeating the colours used to make the fringe.

Pouch Bag

You will need:
100g (4oz) pale green yarn
100g (4oz) emerald yarn
50g (2oz) sage green yarn
Softboard and pins
Crochet hook
Green fabric 137mm × 187mm
(5½in × 7½in) for lining
Needle and green cotton

Length of threads:
2 pale green threads 200mm (8in)
long for thread bearers each end
18 pale green threads 3m (3yd)
long
12 sage green threads 3m (3yd)
long
6 emerald threads 3m (3yd) long
4 emerald threads 500mm (20in)
long for each braid
4 emerald threads 3.25m (3¼yd)
long for each braid
4 emerald threads 1m (1yd) long
for the handle
4 emerald threads 8m (8yd) long
for the handle

Colour sequence:
P = pale green
E = emerald
S = sage green
(read colours from left to
centre, then back again)
PSSP PSSP PSSP PEEP
PE centre

1 Mount threads onto thread bearer. Tie five rows of alternating square knots.

2 The first half of the centre cross pattern, worked in three sections across the bag.

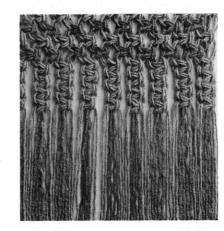

3 Complete the centre pattern, and tie square knot braids in between the centre pattern and the sides.

4 Tie four rows of alternating square knots and nine braids of four square knots each.

5 Four more rows of square knots and one row of hitches complete the first side of the bag.

The bag in this project is ideal for a small purse worn around the neck, or on the shoulder. The wool suggested here is weaving yarn, which is coarser and more tightly spun than knitting wool, and has a slight twist. You could use knitting wool, but this yarn is particularly suitable as it is more hard-wearing — this is worth bearing in mind when you are making something that is going to be handled a lot.

The bag is worked in one piece, folded and hemmed together each side. Follow steps 1–5 to the base, then go back to step 1 for the other side. Finish the knotting by using the other two thread bearers as leaders for a row of hitches, so that each edge will look the same. Trim the ends of the wool and tuck them inside. Fold the macramé right sides together and hem the side seams with matching yarn, using a blunt tapestry needle. Place the two lining pieces right sides together and stitch the side seams. Turn the macramé right side out and insert the lining.

Twist the braids (6) at the side of the bag and pin them in position at the top two corners of the bag. Pin the handles in position by

6 Make two braids of square and half knots. Slot through each side of the bag as shown here.

the side of the braids.

Hem the lining around the top inside edges, trapping the handles and braids under it each side of the bag (7).

Variations
The actual size of the bag shown here is 125 × 175mm (5 × 7in). You could enlarge it by mounting additional groups of 12 threads either side of the 36 indicated here to make a wider bag. Mount the threads in the same colour sequence. For extra length, cut your threads eight times the finished size you want, remembering to add the front and back lengths together as the bag is worked in one piece. You could then repeat the centre cross pattern (2–3) a second time for each side of the bag.

Purse
You could also make a purse in the same way as the bag shown here, with a flap at the front which could be fastened with a button and loop, or a press stud. You would need to work steps 1–5 exactly the same way, but before finishing the edge with a row of horizontal clove hitches, repeat the five rows of alternating square

7 Make a braid of square and half knots for the handle. Sew it to the inside, underneath the lining.

knots and the centre cross pattern (1–3) again, and then finish the edge. This would give you an additional 100mm (4in) in depth, which would fold over the top of the bag to form the flap. The lining and the handles could still be attached in the same way.

Evening bag
The style and scale of this bag would also be equally attractive made up as a more formal evening bag, possibly worked in gold and silver metallic threads, or in shiny black rayon with the addition of jet beads in the braids (see 32, page 12).

For a special occasion, you could make it up in silky crochet cotton (working with double threads) in colours chosen to match or complement your dress. This could be particularly attractive with some floaty summer voile or printed chiffon. The perfect match of colours in a hand-made bag would give it a special designer touch.

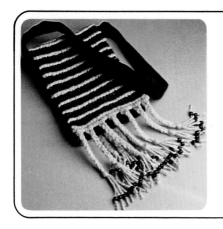

Berber Bag

You will need:
For macramé:
100g (4oz) berber yarn in dark brown
150g (6oz) berber yarn in natural
66 brown wooden beads
Crochet hook

For the bag:
Piece of dark brown hessian
287 × 225mm (11½ × 9in)
For the front of the bag:
2 pieces of dark brown hessian
75 × 750mm (3× 30in)
For the handle and sides of bag:
Needle and brown cotton

Length of threads:
2 natural threads 250mm (10in) long for thread bearers
24 natural threads 5m (5yd) long
5 dark brown threads 5.5m (5½yd) long
21 natural threads 300mm (12in) long for plaits at back
3 natural threads 1m (1yd) long for plait on front edge of bag

The bag in this project is made from hessian material and berber yarn. Berber is the name of a type of yarn which has a coarse, natural quality. The knots used are vertical and horizontal hitches, which are tied to make a

1 Mount 24 threads onto the thread bearer. Tie one row of horizontal hitches. The brown thread is leader.

2 Two rows of vertical hitches complete the pattern. Repeat eight more times.

3 Tie one row of horizontal hitches, two more pattern steps and a row of horizontal hitches.

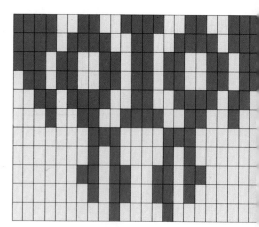

4 This pattern consists of horizontal and vertical hitches in 11 rows. Decrease either side.

5 When you have completed the pattern, tie two horizontal hitch rows diagonally towards the centre.

6 Make plaits with the centre 12 threads 200mm (8in) long. Darn the rest inside. Add beads.

7 Hook threads into the top edge and make seven plaits 125mm (5in) long. Add beads.

bold contrasting pattern.

Mount the threads onto thread bearers and follow the steps, tying the knots with single threads as this yarn is fairly thick. The bag is worked from the back to the front flap. Use the dark brown threads as leaders and to tie vertical hitches. When you run out of a brown thread, tuck the end behind and loop another round the next natural thread and continue. Darn the ends in later. Follow the diagram for the pattern on the front of the bag, working across in rows from side to side. Make plaits of three threads each, using the remaining centre 12 threads on the front. The rest are darned inside. Mount 21 threads on the other end for seven plaits.

To complete the bag, turn in a hem on the piece of hessian to be the front. Join the two long strips of hessian, fold lengthwise and hem to make the sides and strap. Then, with the join at the base, hem this strip to the hessian front and macramé back of bag. Edge the front with a plait of natural berber yarn.

Jewelry

1 Tie an overhand knot 62mm (2½in) from the end with all threads, then two square knots.

2 Put beads as shown, and repeat the pattern of square knots and beads six more times.

PURPLE NECKLACE

You will need:
25g (1oz) maroon cotton
30 purple beads
64 small pink beads
Softboard and pins

Length of threads:
6 threads 3.5m (3½yd) long

There are many ways of making jewelry simply and effectively with macramé. This purple necklace could easily be made in an hour or two. It is made of cotton, and the actual size is 1m (1yd).

Begin by tying all six threads together in an overhand knot 62mm (2½in) from the ends. Pin through this knot to your softboard. Tie two square knots and then divide the six threads into two groups. Put a pink bead onto a single thread, a purple bead onto all three threads, and then another pink bead. Put beads on the other threads in the same way. This pattern is repeated until there are seven groups of beads altogether. The centre of the necklace consists of four square knots either side of a group of beads (3). The pattern is then repeated seven more times. Tie a second overhand knot with all the threads, and trim the ends to 62mm (2½in) from the knot to finish off.

Variations
There are several variations of the necklace which you might like to try. Instead of the square knots between the groups of beads, you could tie half knots of one of the alternating chains in Sampler One (pages 8–13). Other equally attractive knots shown in Sampler Two (pages 33–37) are the square knot with loops and the Josephine knot. Silk, rayon or linen threads with small beads would make a very delicate chain necklace.

BLACK PENDANT

You will need:
25g (1oz) fine black crochet cotton
8 small black beads
12 medium round black beads
4 large black jet beads
Softboard and pins

Length of threads:
14 threads 750mm (30in) long
6 threads 750mm (30in) long to hang pendant

Place 12 of the threads flat in an inverted U shape. Pin them to the board at the centre top. Put four small beads on the outer threads, then lay the remaining two threads horizontally across, below the beads, as leaders. Tie a row of horizontal hitches and add two more beads. Tie four rows of diagonal hitches on each side, with the threads in pairs, and put a larger bead on the centre two.

The next pattern is a diamond of three rows of diagonal hitches out from the centre, then two rows inwards again. Finish with two more diagonal hitch rows, then put beads on each end. Secure with overhand knots.

The pendant hangs from six threads looped through the centre top, or you could put it on a velvet ribbon to wear as a choker.

Variations

Two more pieces of macramé jewelry are shown here. First is a delicate band of metallic silver thread and glass beads with matching earrings. The knots are square knot braids with tiny round glass and bronze beads, and long bugles.

The necklace consists of eight lengths of silver thread which you would place flat on your working board in the same formation as you see in the picture, with four threads leading to the middle from each side and down to the ends at the centre front. You would need to cut the thread to six times the required finished length. Tie the two groups together in the centre to begin with, working down the centre front. Then, working out from the centre pattern on each side, tie each group of four threads together with square knots at the ends and attach to the fastenings.

The earrings are part of the pattern in the centre front.

3 Centre pattern consists of five square knots, ten beads and five more square knots.

4 After the centre pattern, repeat step 2 of pattern another seven times. End with an overhand knot.

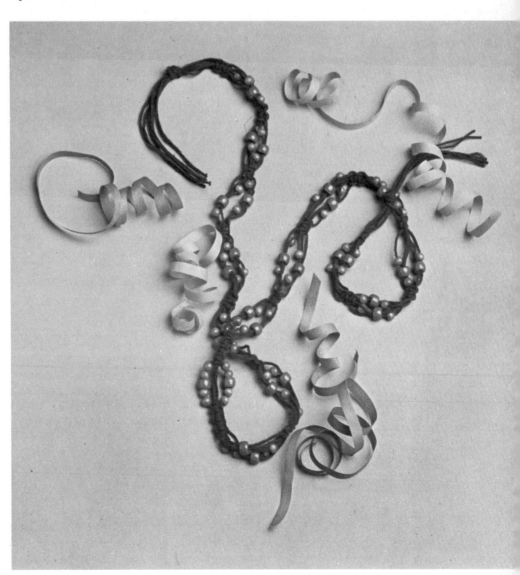

The pendant of ceramic stones and cream crochet thread is another simple and effective accessory that is easily made. You can find unusual and attractive stones on the beach, or in a shop specializing in semi-precious stones and shells. Ceramic beads can be made from instant clay which is easy to model — there are several types available which do not require firing. Wooden pendants would also make attractive jewelry combined with macramé. The setting for the stones shown here consists of half and square knot braids.

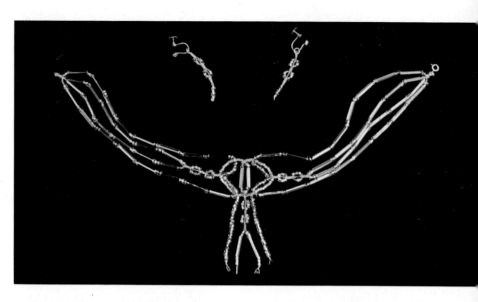

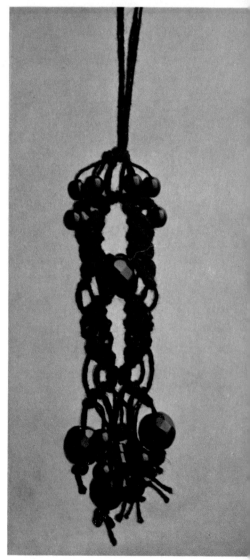

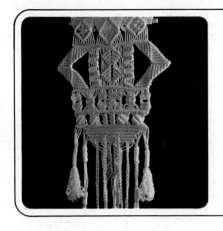

Sampler Two

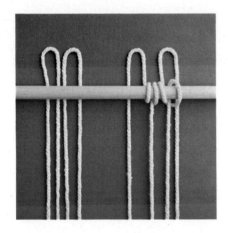

1 Square knot mount. Put two loops behind the dowel and tie clove hitches with inner threads.

2 Tie a square knot with two outer threads and attach it to the dowel with clove hitches.

3 Clove hitch mount. The four steps shown here make a picot edge above the dowel.

You will need:
300g (¾lb) cotton string
Piece of dowel 12 × 225mm
(½ × 9in)
Softboard and pins
Elastic bands

Length of threads:
20 threads 8m (8yd) long

This project gives instructions on a second sampler which is the same size as the first, and again made of white cotton string. It will introduce you to some new and slightly more intricate knots, plus some variations of the first basic

knots given in Sampler One (pages 8–13). Again each varying pattern is divided by a complete row of horizontal hitches.

First of all there is a variation in the way the threads are mounted. The centre 16 threads form four clove hitch mounts which make a decorative picot above the dowel. Either side are two looped square knot mounts consisting of four threads each (1–3).

The first section of the sampler is made up of square knot braids, all slightly more decorative versions of the basic square knot braid. The most central one (4),

has another variation, not shown, which is easy to do. When you have tied a square knot, spaced a little down the centre threads, instead of pushing the knot upwards, leave it in its place and continue with the next knot. This braid is shown on pages 53–54, in the Macramé Blind.

The next section uses alternating square knot patterns, and a bobble with the same knot. Remember to tie a knot immediately below the bobble very tightly before continuing. You can also make an alternating pattern of bobbles, as you would

33

with square knots.

The third and four sections show more ways of using the vertical and horizontal hitches. As these patterns are symmetrical and made up of various angles, use pins frequently to keep the knots in their correct positions.

In both samplers the various knots are worked in single motifs or small areas of repeats. It is worth noting here that a piece of macramé can be built up from just two or three repeating shapes to give a very attractive effect. The clove hitch is a particularly good knot for this, as it has a very pleasing simplicity. Some of the most striking macramé hangings consist of only one knot used with many coloured threads, or, conversely, two or three repeating patterns in only one type of thread. Having learned how to tie the knots, you may want to go on to designing your own pieces of macramé. If it is to be a decorative piece, choose the type of thread you like and use knots suitable for it. If it is to be functional, choose the kind of materials that will suit its purpose.

In the last part of the sampler you will be learning some new knots. First the Josephine knot, which is based on the interlocking of two threads to make a pattern like a figure of eight. You can use two single threads or two pairs, as shown here, or you can use two groups of threads if you want a larger knot.

The Josephine knot is perfect for making table or floor mats as it lies very flat, and has an extremely elegant and fluid pattern. You could try working it in very thick cord or even rope to make a mat.

In contrast, the berry knot is a spherical-shaped knot, consisting of diagonal clove hitches pulled into shape with square knots tied very tightly.

4 Two square knot braids. On the left, space each knot to slide up the centre threads and form a loop.

5 This lacy square knot uses eight threads. Begin with centre threads CDEF, then BDEG and ADEH.

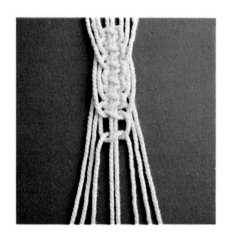

6 Now reverse the pattern tying threads ADEH again, then BDEG and finally CDEF.

7 The square knot braid shown here is tied by alternating the inner and outer threads for each knot.

8 The square knot bobble. Tie five square knots. Put centre threads over the top. Tie below bobble.

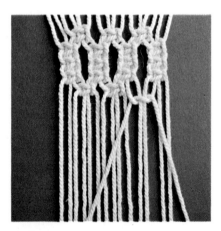

9 Another alternating square knot pattern. One row of three knots, one row of single knots.

10 Detail of the sampler at this stage with one row of horizontal hitches to complete the pattern.

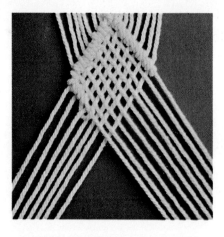

11 This attractive diamond pattern has centre threads which are woven over and under each other.

12 Another diamond with a square knot of eight threads tied in the centre.

13 Four square knots are tied within this diamond in an alternating pattern.

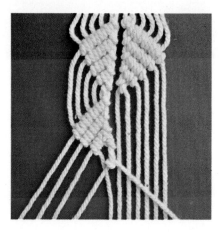

14 Tie five rows of diagonal hitches. Leave the last thread free on each row to form a triangle.

15 A simple and effective braid of horizontal hitches, tied diagonally over six threads.

16 Angular patterns can be made like this with vertical hitches. Work from left to right.

17 Turn the sampler on its side. Repeat step 16, working from right to left in the same way.

18 Turn the sampler upright, then on its side, repeating the pattern until you have an angle like this.

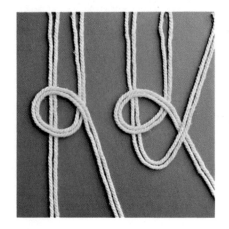

19 The first steps of the Josephine knot, a rather more intricate knot, but a graceful one.

20 The second steps shown here complete the knot. It can also begin with the left threads over the right.

21 The sampler so far. Note the importance of the horizontal hitches dividing each pattern.

22 The berry knot. Tie two square knots, then four diagonal rows of hitches.

23 Tie a square knot below the hitches on the right. Pull it very tight. Repeat on the left.

24 Tie six rows of hitches, decreasing on each row. Plait the free threads on row 4.

25 The free threads on row 6 are now plaited. Repeat step 14 to make the pattern below.

26 Coiling. Wind the left thread upwards around the others. Pull this thread down on the inside.

27 Finish the sampler with coils, as shown here and fringe the ends of all the threads. Trim.

Cushion

You will need:

For the macramé:
100g (4oz) rust yarn
100g (4oz) burgundy yarn
Softboard and pins
Crochet hook

For the cushion:
Piece of dark brown needlecord
750mm × 1.5m (¾ × 1½yd)
Kapok or foam filling
Needle and brown cotton

Length of threads:

36 burgundy threads 1m (1yd) long
2 burgundy threads 250mm (10in) long as thread bearers
2 burgundy threads 250mm (10in) long as leaders
8 rust threads 6m (6yd) long
4 burgundy threads 375mm (15in) long for each shorter plait
2 rust threads 375mm (15in) long for each shorter plait
4 burgundy threads 500mm (20in) long for each longer plait
2 rust threads 500mm (20in) long for each longer plait

The cushion on these pages shows how you can create a tapestry effect by using a combination of vertical and horizontal clove hitches and coloured yarn. The

1 Mount burgundy threads onto two of the thread bearers.

2 Introduce a rust thread to the left edge with a lark's head.

3 Tie three rows of vertical hitches across all burgundy threads, ending on right edge.

4 Following the pattern, tie vertical hitches with rust, and horizontal hitches with burgundy.

cushion shown here is 325mm (13in) square.

First, mount the burgundy threads on the two thread bearers with lark's head knots (1). You will be using the threads in pairs to give an added thickness to the knots. Both kinds of hitches are worked across from edge to edge in complete rows, starting at top left. The rust threads are introduced during the working of the knots as required, and act as tying threads for vertical hitches, showing as rust, and as leaders for horizontal hitches, showing as burgundy. When you run out of a rust thread, tuck the end towards the back, and mount another on the next burgundy thread along.

To begin the knots, mount a rust thread (2). Tie one clove hitch immediately below the lark's head and continue across (3). Change from vertical to horizontal hitches as indicated in the diagram, the dark squares being horizontal hitches. There are 31 rows in all, the centre one being the sixteenth. After the last row, lay two burgundy leaders across and tie a horizontal hitch row, so that the top and bottom edges look the same. Trim the threads to 25mm (1in), turn under and sew down with brown cotton. Turn under the remaining ends of the thread bearers and leaders, and sew. Make the cushion from needlecord or velvet, and fill with kapok or foam. Sew the macramé to the centre of the cushion.

Finally, make four plaits (6) to trim the edges of the macramé, and four longer plaits to sew to the edges of the cushion, as shown in the big picture.

Variations
This pattern could be equally attractive used on a seat for an upright chair, or as a bag backed in matching fabric.

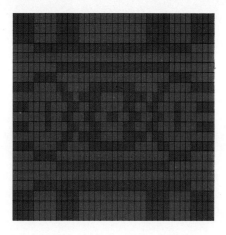

5 Diagram of the pattern. Each dark square represents a horizontal clove hitch.

6 Make four plaits 250mm (10in) long and four plaits 350mm (14in) long for edging the cushion.

Table Mats

You will need:
For the plaits:
300g (¾lb) natural jute
200g (½lb) yellow jute
Softboard and pins
Tape measure

For the lining:
2 pieces of natural linen fabric
300mm × 250mm (12 × 10in)
Needle and cotton

Length of threads:
For each mat:
48 natural threads 1m (1yd) long
30 yellow threads 1m (1yd) long
2 natural threads 300mm (12in)
long for leaders

Lay threads flat on the board
before you begin to make the
plaits. There are ten plaits
altogether, eight of which consist
of three natural threads each, and
these are the widest. Then there
are two narrower plaits of three
yellow threads each, which are
positioned immediately in from
the wide plait on each edge.

Having placed your threads in
their correct order, lay the first
natural leader across all threads,
50mm (2in) from the top edge.
Working from left to right, tie a
row of horizontal hitches. This

1 Lay one of the leader threads
across all the threads and tie one row
of horizontal hitches.

2 Divide the threads into 10 groups
and plait each group for 262mm
(10½in).

3 Lay a second leader across the
threads immediately below the plaits.
Tie a row of hitches to finish edge.

4 Trim ends to 50mm (2in) to make
fringes and fray. Sew linen fabric to
the back of each mat.

row then serves as an edge to the mat, and the ends above it form the fringe. It will help you to tie an overhand knot at each end of the leader, and pin down through each knot to the board, so that the leader stays in position while you are tying a clove hitch knot with each thread.

Now plait each group of yellow and natural threads for 262mm (10½in) and make two narrow plaits with each group of three yellow threads.

To complete the other edge of the mat, lay the second leader across all the threads below the plaits and tie a second row of hitches.

Trim the ends to 50mm (2in). Fray the jute each end for the fringes. Turn the remaining ends of the leaders in at the back, hem flat and trim.

The mats are finished with a backing of natural linen fabric. Make a 12mm (½in) turning to the inside, and hem around the edges with matching cotton. From the front of each mat, sew the plaits to the linen with small running stitches, taking care that your sewing does not show or pull the plaits tight (4). It may be a good idea to press the mats when they are complete to make sure they are really flat.

Materials
The jute illustrated here is a coarse and rather hairy type of string, which you are most likely to find in a hardware or gardening shop. It was chosen for its hard-wearing ability which is important for something which is essentially functional. It is, in fact, very supple, so is not at all difficult to knot. It also has an attractive natural look to it.

You will find that coloured jute is usually available, but you may want to dye it yourself to a particular shade. The yellow jute here was hand-dyed in a cold water dye, and as yellow is a fairly pale colour the jute was bleached first to absorb the dye more easily. For deeper colours, this would not be necessary.

Other materials suitable for the mats would be cotton string or linen threads, as long as they were the right thickness and fairly flexible. There are many polypropylene and nylon mixtures on the market, but bear in mind that the mats may need to be heat-resistant, so choose any of those with care.

Variations
By enlarging the same design you could make runners for your sideboard or tray cloths to match the table mats. You could also make mats or runners for the dressing table to the same design. Use cotton, silk or linen thread for a more delicate effect, and choose or dye a colour to match your bedroom furnishings.

Kaftan

You will need:
50g (2oz) lilac bouclé wool
50g (2oz) red bouclé wool
50g (2oz) maroon bouclé wool
Softboard and pins
Crochet hook
Needle and cottons to match wool
Commercial paper pattern and fabric for kaftan

Length of threads:
For yoke of kaftan, each edge:
6 lilac threads 3m (3yd) long
4 red threads 3m (3yd) long
4 maroon threads 3m (3yd) long
1 lilac thread 200mm (8in) long as thread bearer
For each sleeve of kaftan:
1 red thread 2.5m (2½yd) long
1 lilac thread 2.5m (2½yd) long

Colour sequence:
L = lilac
R = red
M = maroon
LL RR MM LL MM RR LL
AB CD EF   GH JK   LM NP

The kaftan in this section is given a decorative and individual quality by the addition of macramé braids. Make a kaftan from a pattern of your own choice, possibly similar to this one with a yoke and wide sleeves. The

1 Tie a square knot with centre threads FGHJ. Keep G and H at the centre. Tie a knot with EGHK.

2 Tie two more square knots, first with DGHL and then CGHM, to form the central pattern.

3 Tie two more square knots, first with BGHN, then AGHP. Repeat with AGHP.

4 Working out from centre, tie a square knot with BGHN. The outer threads begin to curve.

lengths of the threads given here are for a yoke measuring 350mm (14in) from the shoulders, and sleeves 450mm (18in) at the hem. To find the correct lengths for your kaftan, take the measurements for yoke and sleeves, and multiply by eight.

Mount the threads in colour sequence. They are lettered to help you when tying the knots. The pattern is a square knot braid, which is shown in step 5 of the second sampler, but in this case you are using 14 threads.

Work on a board, and follow steps 1–5. To make the ribbons for the front, and the maroon edging on the yoke, tie the lilac, red and maroon threads nearest to the centre of the yoke in alternating chains, using each pair of the colours. Hook the remaining threads onto the back of the braid and trim. Make the braid for the other side of the yoke in the same way, again making ribbons of the three colours nearest to the centre.

Sew the macramé to the yoke using matching cottons, then place the maroon threads nearest the centre along the edges of the front yoke. Sew in place, tucking the ends under the braids at the top.

The sleeves are edged with lilac and red braids of alternating chains. Begin from the centre of each thread, as shown in step 1 (page 50), in the project for applied macramé on curtains.

Variations

You could make finer braids of silk or rayon, mounted onto a silk or crepe fabric, and if the macramé braids were soft enough they could also be applied round the hem. The most important thing to bear in mind is the weight of the threads in relation to the weight of the fabric.

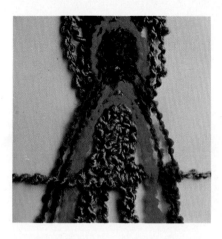

5 Continue with red and maroon threads. Steps 1 to 5 form the pattern, and are repeated.

6 Lay a lilac thread across the ends, and tie a row of horizontal hitches to finish the edge.

Silk Scarf and Bag

You will need:
Softboard and pins
Tape measure
Needle and pink cotton

For the bag:
25g (1oz) pink crochet cotton
50g (2oz) pale grey rayon or silk thread
Piece of pink silk 400 × 137mm (16 × 5½in) for lining
2 pieces pink silk 300 × 37mm (12 × 1½in) for drawstrings

For the scarf:
20g (¾oz) pink crochet cotton
25g (1oz) pale grey rayon or silk thread
Piece of silk 1.5m × 200mm (1½yd × 8in)

Length of threads:
For the bag:
2 pink threads 200mm (8in) long as thread bearers
10 pink threads 2.5m (2½yd) long
18 grey threads 2.5m (2½yd) long

For the scarf:
2 pink threads 255mm (9in) long as thread bearers
12 pink threads 550mm (22in)
24 grey threads 550mm (22in)

BAG

Colour sequence:
G = pale grey
P = pink
GGGG GPPG GPPG GPPG
GPPG GPPG GGGG

The bag is made in one piece, so follow steps 1–4 and work back for the other side. Finish off the edges of the knots by trimming the ends and turning them to the inside. Hem the sides together.

To make the lining, stitch 12mm (½in) side seams and turn down 35mm (1½in) at the top. Sew two lines (6). Open the side seams between the lines.

For the drawstrings, fold in the edges of the two pieces of silk 6mm (¼in), then fold in half again and stitch. Thread once handle through the top of the silk lining, between the stitched lines, from one side all round and out again. Slot in the second handle from the other side, round in the opposite direction. Put the lining inside the macramé, and hem.

SCARF

Make the fringes for the scarf separately (7).

1 Tie seven braids of eight square knots each, and one alternate row of pink knots.

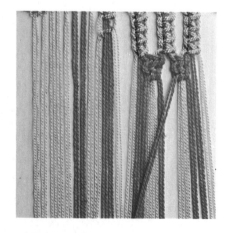

2 Tie seven braids of four square knots each, and one alternate row of two pink knots.

44

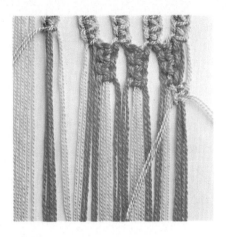

3 Tie seven braids of four square knots again, and an alternate row of three pink knots.

4 Tie seven braids of two square knots to complete this side of bag. Repeat steps 4–1.

5 Lay a pink thread across, and tie a row of hitches to finish the edge. Trim ends. Hem back on the inside.

6 Sew two lines 25mm (1in) apart at the top. Thread in the two handles in opposite directions.

7 The fringe on the scarf is 10 braids of four square knots and an alternate row of pink knots.

Suede Macramé

You will need:
Suede thongs 6mm (¼in) wide in various colours
Softboard and bulldog clips
Glue suitable for leather

Length of threads:
For braids of Josephine knots cut thongs five times the actual length required
For braids of alternating chains, cut thongs five times the actual length required
For braids of square knots cut thongs eight times the actual length required

Suede has a naturally soft and flexible quality which is very suitable for macramé. Thongs should be cut thinly to enable you to tie knots easily, and as they need to be fairly long for braids, cut several lengths and glue them together by overlapping the ends.

Belt
For the belt shown (above) you will need a band of green suede 25mm (1 in) wide. The length should be half your waist size. Calculate the total length your belt would need to be when tied, and cut the thongs as indicated

above. Glue two green and two turquoise thongs to each end of the band. Use the clips to hold the suede firmly to the board while you are working. Try to arrange the colours neatly in the Josephine knots (1).

You could make a belt entirely of Josephine knots, in which case the length of the thongs should be five times your waist size, plus ends for tying at the front. For a wider belt, use two or more groups of four thongs for each Josephine knot braid. Loop the outer thongs of each group around the adjacent ones in the

1 The Josephine knot, using two colours for the belt. Arrange the colours neatly.

2 Alternating chains for the jacket. A combination of colours adds to their attractive quality.

3 Two more braids. Spaced square knots with loops on the left, and double alternating chains.

spaces between the knots, to hold the braids together.

Another idea you might like to try for a slightly heavier type of belt would be to make a braid of Josephine knots of the required length, and then to mount it onto a band of leather. Put a little glue behind each knot and press firmly onto the leather. The thongs would need to extend beyond the ends of the leather to tie at the front.

Take care when using the glue to apply it sparingly, or it may spread onto the suede and mark it.

JACKET

Here is an illustration of how macramé braids can enhance a simple jacket. Make your jacket from a commercial pattern, using suede, as shown here, or a velvet, corduroy or woollen fabric.

The braids which form the edging are single alternating chains made with two suede thongs of contrasting colours (2). Measure the lengths of the front and pocket edges and cut the thongs as indicated above. Fix them in position with a leather glue, or sew them with a cobbler's needle and thread.

Variations

Several of the braids shown in Samplers One and Two can be made using suede, and step 3 gives two examples. The suedes in this project are a fairly supple kind called 'suede splits', which have a suede face on each side. Soft leather, such as glove or pigskin, would be equally suitable for knots, and suede and glove leather come in a variety of bright and subtle colours. Chamois leather is not so successful when cut into narrow small pieces as it tends to stretch and lose its shape.

Basket

You will need:
5.5m (5½yd) natural rope 6mm (¼in) thick
150g (6oz) natural jute
Brass or steel ring 12mm (½in) in diameter
Softboard and pins
Carpet needle
Crochet hook

Length of threads:
84 jute threads 1.5m (1½yd) long

Another aspect of macramé is working in three dimensions, and the basket shown here is an introduction to tying and shaping knots into a definite form. It is also different from the other projects in that it is worked from the centre in a circle. You will need a small metal ring, such as a curtain ring, for the middle of the basket.

Take 26 of the jute threads and mount them onto the ring with lark's head knots. Pin the ring firmly to the board and place the beginning of the rope against it. Tie a complete round of horizontal hitches with the threads over the rope. The jute used here is fairly fine, so the threads are knotted in pairs. If the jute you use is thicker, take a single thread for each clove hitch.

After the first round, continue into the second, and as you are increasing add an extra thread after every three of the original ones you mounted. Do this by mounting each thread onto the rope with a lark's head as you work round. The rope can be positioned very slightly apart from the first round of hitches.

Continue increasing by adding an extra thread after every two on the third round, and between each one on the fourth. Carry on making complete rounds until you have 10 altogether. Add

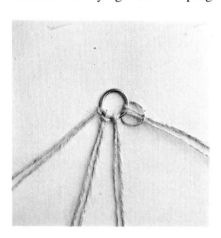

1 Mount 26 threads onto the ring with lark's head knots so that it is completely covered.

2 Pin the rope over the threads close to the ring. Tie horizontal hitches with each pair of threads.

3 Complete the first round. On the second round, mount an extra thread on the rope after every three threads.

48

threads to the rope where necessary.

On the eleventh round, place the rope directly above the previous one, pulling the hitches very tight to hold it firm. This is to give a rim to the basket. In the twelfth and last round, make the handles by looping the rope for about 75mm (3in) on each side, and only tie clove hitches either side of the loops (4).

If you have difficulty keeping the basket in shape, it might help if you place it over something round while you are working on it, so that you are almost working on a mould.

Finishing

The basket is finished by hooking all the threads through to the back. Take each one in turn and pull it over the rim and down just inside it. This will help to hold the rim in place. Now tie threads in pairs with overhand knots. Hem them flat with a needle and jute thread, and trim the ends close to the stitching (5).

Variations

To make a basket with a much deeper rim, begin with a longer piece of rope and simply continue tying more rounds up the side. The ends can then be hooked through to the inside of the rim and finished off in the same way.

For other baskets, choose your materials according to the type of basket you want to make. For example, a sewing basket could be made of the same jute as is shown here, with a rim about 125mm (5in) deep. You could also make a lid to match, following the same method of tying flat rounds.

A log basket would need to be made of much thicker rope and coarse string such as sisal or hemp.

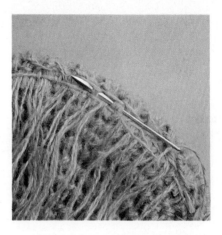

4 On rows 11 and 12, place the rope immediately above the tenth round. Pull the hitches tight to form rim.

5 Hook the ends to back of basket, tie in pairs, and hem down with needle and jute. Trim.

Applied Macramé

You will need:

For macramé braids:
50g (2oz) orange 2-ply rug yarn
50g (2oz) mustard 2-ply rug yarn
50g (2oz) dark brown 2-ply rug yarn
Softboard and pins
Needle and cotton to match yarns

For curtains:
Unbleached calico

Length of threads:

For alternating chain braids:
Orange 1: 2 orange threads
12.5m (12½yd) long
Orange 2: 2 orange threads 6.5m
(6½yd) long
Brown 1: 2 brown threads 5.5m
(5½yd) long

For square knot braids:
Orange and brown: 2 orange
threads 11.75 (11¾yd) long and
2 brown threads 11.75m
(11¾yd) long
Mustard: 4 mustard threads
12.25 (12¼yd) long
Brown 2: 4 brown threads
11.75m (11¾yd) long

CURTAINS

The actual size of the design
illustrated here is 750mm ×

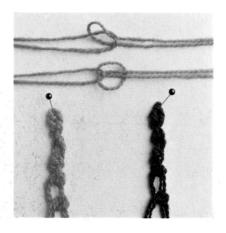

1 Alternating chains. Loop the centre of one thread through the other in a lark's head knot.

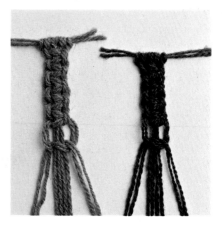

2 Square knot braids, mounted on a thread bearer with the lark's head knot.

3 Square knot braids using two colours. Mount in the order shown here.

4 Pin the braids in place on the curtain before sewing down with matching cottons.

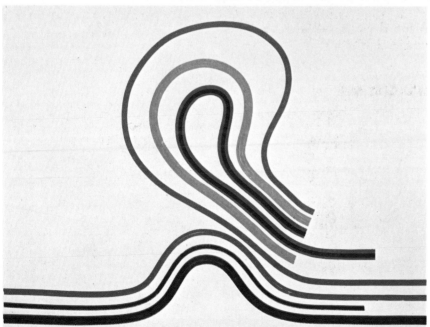

5 Diagram of the pattern.

1.25m (30in × 1¼yd) for each curtain. If you want your design to be a different size to fit the curtains you are making, you will need to work out the length of threads you require. First draw out your design to actual size, and measure each line. For a line which will be an alternating chain, multiply its length by five. You will need two threads for each chain. For a square knot braid, measure the line and multiply its length by eight. You will need four threads for each braid, and a 50mm (2in) length for the thread bearer.

Variations

There are many ways in which you could use applied macramé apart from the curtains you see illustrated here. You could apply a decorative edging to chair-covers or cushions, or you could make braids as a fashion feature to put on the hem of a shirt, to edge the front of a jerkin or to decorate pockets or cuffs on a dress.

You might want to try working in a variety of materials, such as cotton, silk or rayon thread for something delicate, or wool or furnishing cord for a thicker,

wider braid. If you wanted to make a more elaborate pattern, you could also try a combination of different braids and threads for a richer effect.

CUSHION

The cushion shown here has an applied pattern of braids made in the same rug yarn as the curtains. The braids used are alternating chains, tied with two and four threads, as in the first sampler. They are measured and sewn on in the same way as the curtains, using matching cottons.

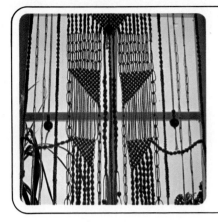

Macramé Blind

You will need:

500g (1lb) cotton string
Piece of dowel 550mm (22in) long × 12mm (½in) diameter
22 round wooden beads 25mm (1in) across
56 wooden beads 12mm (½in) across

Length of threads:

For the centre area:
44 threads 8m (8yd) long
For each side, beginning from threads next to centre area:
4 threads 8m (8yd) long
4 threads 500mm (½yd) long
8 threads 1.75m (1¾yd) long
4 threads 8m (8yd) long
For each braid to hang the screen:
4 threads 750mm (¾yd) long
For the centre top:
2 threads 400mm (16in) long

The blind in this project is a good example of macramé creating an equal balance between function and decoration. The delicate shapes made by the knots are shown to their best advantage when hanging against a window with the light shining through, and the blind can cast fascinating patterns of sunlight and shadow in a room.

Carry out the knots by concentrating first on the centre area. The 44 threads you mount on the dowel first are taken singly, so this area will in fact consist of 88 threads in all.

Follow steps 1–6 initially, then work the threads either side (7, 8), and finish the ends with beads (9).

The first pattern at the top is the large triangle of alternating square knots. Work in rows from side to side, decreasing two threads at the beginning and end of each row. The threads from each edge are then tied in half and

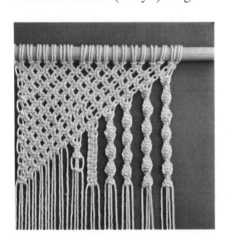

1 Tie a triangular shape of alternating square knots and nine square and half knot braids.

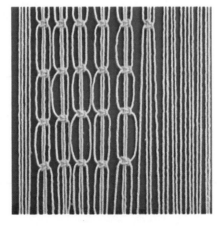

2 Continue with nine spaced square knot braids 100mm (4in) long, then make another triangle.

3 The blind so far. Tie a half knot braid at the centre and wrap the four threads each side.

square knot braids to end level with the tip of the triangle (1).

The centre area can then be divided in half. The three middle groups of four threads hang free, with wrapping, half and square knot braids. Either side of them are nine spaced square knots and another triangle (2 and 3).

Note that the four inner and outer threads from the second triangles now hang down in spaced square knots.

Complete the centre area with two more small triangles, each of 28 threads, and seven half knot braids below them (4, 5).

The three centre braids should end level with the tips of the third triangles. Add the small beads before trimming the ends.

Now tie the braids either side of the centre (6, 7).

Complete the blind with beads and overhand knots to secure them (9). Trim the ends of all the threads. Mount the threads for hanging the blind on each end of the dowel and tie 12 square knots, leave a small loop, then tie an overhand knot.

Add two remaining threads 400mm (16in) long to the exact centre of the blind, and attach a large bead to the ends.

Variations

You may want to make a blind to fit a particular window, in which case you could easily add or subtract the number of braids on either side, and adjust the length accordingly. The actual size of the blind shown here is 1m × 525mm (1yd × 21in).

The delicate open pattern of the blind would also look attractive as a room divider, or as a screen where the light needed to show through. Wooden dowels or brass rods at the top and bottom would make a neater rectangular shape.

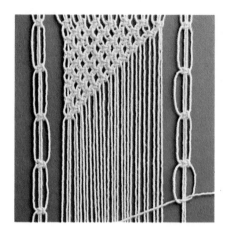

4 87mm (3½in) below the tip of the second triangle, tie a third triangle with only 28 threads.

5 Tie eight half knot braids below the triangle. The outer braids loop across to the edges.

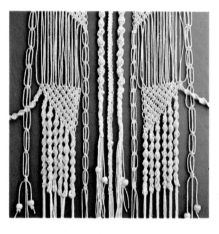

6 The blind at this stage. The centre braid is now square knots. Wrap the threads each side.

7 At the sides of the centre area, tie half and square knot braids as shown here.

8 Join half knot looped braids to the outer braids. Put beads on the ends of the threads and secure.

9 Put beads on the ends of the centre area. Trim all the ends below the beads evenly.

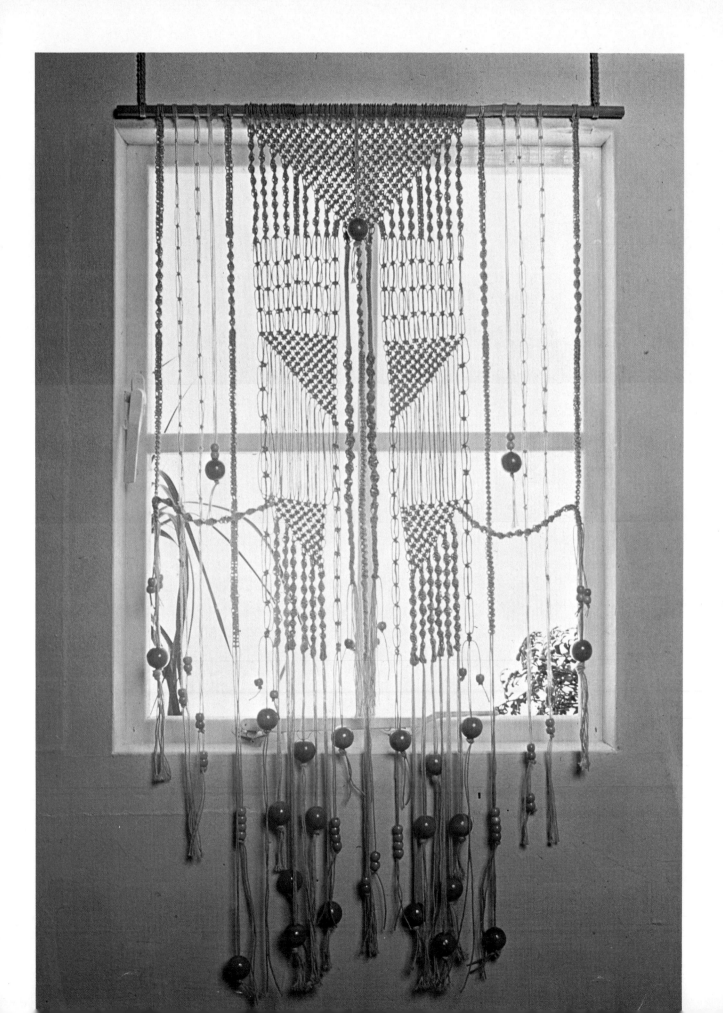

Picture

You will need:

For the macramé picture:
50g (2oz) turquoise 2-ply rug yarn
Oddments of rug yarn in the following colours:
White, cream, grey, light brown, dark brown, black, rust, dark green, yellow ochre

For mounting the finished picture:
Piece of cream mounting board
412 × 275mm (16½ × 11in)
2 pieces of wooden beading
12mm (½in) wide and 412mm (16½in) long
2 pieces of beading 250mm (10in) long
Strong glue
Piece of mounting board
100 × 50mm (4 × 2in) and string to hang the picture

Length of threads:

35 turquoise threads 1m (1yd) long
2 turquoise threads 300mm (12in) long as thread bearers
Rug yarn in assorted colours as indicated above including turquoise, in approximately 2m (2yd) lengths

The project on these pages shows how you can interpret a picture

1 Mount all threads and introduce a turquoise thread on left side. Tie nine vertical hitch rows.

2 Row 10. Work to twenty-second thread from right side, turn, and decrease to fifteenth thread.

3 Having completed turquoise area, introduce threads of different colours on left side of picture.

4 The white area is worked after you have completed the knots on the left side of the picture.

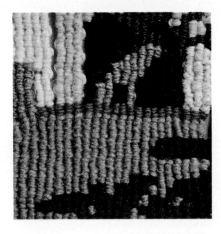

5 Continue working on the left side of the picture, following on from the white area in step 4.

6 The centre right area, tying hitches to depict the tree and the courtyard behind it.

7 Complete the tree and the shadows on the ground at the bottom of the picture.

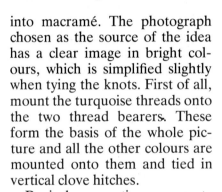

into macramé. The photograph chosen as the source of the idea has a clear image in bright colours, which is simplified slightly when tying the knots. First of all, mount the turquoise threads onto the two thread bearers. These form the basis of the whole picture and all the other colours are mounted onto them and tied in vertical clove hitches.

Begin by mounting a separate length of turquoise yarn onto the first left thread with a lark's head knot (1). Tie vertical hitches for nine rows. Step 2 shows how to begin decreasing the turquoise area by turning around in the middle of the threads and working back. The rest of the steps then show how to progress through the different parts of the picture by concentrating on those areas in turn.

To finish, tuck the remaining turquoise threads under, and glue the picture to the board. Edge the board with wooden beading and fix a string loop on the back.

Wall Hanging

1 Mount the centre 26 threads on the small cane. Tie nine diagonal clove hitch rows and two alternating chains.

2 Mount 15 threads either side of the centre. Tie alternating chains and a diagonal clove hitch braid.

You will need:
20g (³/₄oz) each of:
Fine jute string
Cream chenille
White cotton gimp
Turquoise 2-ply rug yarn
Black knitting wool
Yellow knitting wool

Piece of cane 500mm (20in) long and 6mm (¼in) thick shaped into an arc
Piece of cane 1m (1yd) long and 6mm (¼in) thick in a larger arc
19 small corks with holes pierced through the centres
Piece of dowel 100mm (4in) long and 6mm (¼in) thick

Length of threads:
Cut 8m (8yd) lengths:
12 jute
18 chenille
16 cotton gimp
6 turquoise yarn
10 black wool
and also:
4 yellow threads 7.5m (7½yd) long
4 yellow threads 4m (4yd) long
2 turquoise threads 4m (4yd) long
2 jute threads 4m (4yd) long

Colour sequence:
The first group of threads listed above are mounted onto the shorter cane in the following order
(read from left to centre and back again for right half):
J = Jute
C = Chenille
W = Cotton
T = Turquoise
B = Black
WWWWCCJCBBWJCCCCJJW
WTTBBJJCC
BWT centre

Making wall hangings in macramé can be as creative as you want, and once you have a good vocabulary of knots, you can gain as much satisfaction from making and looking at them as you would from a painting.

Mount the 7.5m (7½yd) long yellow threads on the second cane, either side of the centre group (3). Mount the 4m (4yd) long threads onto the small dowel in the middle of the hanging (5).

Mount the centre 26 threads on the shorter cane in the correct order. Tie diagonal clove hitches (1). You will probably find it easier to attach some spare strings to the ends of the cane so that you can hang it on the wall to work on, as it is rather large to put on a board. Now mount 12 more threads either side of the centre group and tie them with knots (2). The threads are all worked in pairs to give added thickness to the knots.

The second cane is introduced by looping the threads around it twice, below the knots already tied. Add two yellow threads either side of the centre area onto the cane. Work down the centre* area first, then tie rows of diagonal hitches with the threads either side as in steps 3 and 4.

Step 5 shows how a small dowel is added with the 4m (4yd) lengths of turquoise, yellow and jute threads mounted on it. The dowel is held in place by the outer two jute threads from the knots above. The jute threads of alternating chains then loop outwards to the sides.

Continue the centre area with the addition of a cork on the middle turquoise threads, and then tie seven rows of diagonal hitches outwards from below the cork.

Finish off all the ends as shown, some with alternating chains, and some with corks (7 and 8). Suspend the hanging from chenille threads which are looped up from each end of the canes to the top. The actual size of the finished hanging is 1.5m (1½ yd) long by 500mm (20in) wide.

Variations

As you can see, it is possible to use completely different types of yarns in one hanging. If you look for contrast in the texture of materials you choose, you will give your hangings additional surface quality. This, combined with the patterns made by the various colours as they move across the hanging, makes macramé come alive.

3 Loop each thread twice round the second cane. Tie more chains and diagonal hitches in centre area.

4 Loop threads around the cane in the same way with two outer groups, and tie knots.

5 The small dowel has eight new threads mounted on it. The jute chains are looped to side groups.

6 Finish the centre area with seven rows of diagonal hitches from below the cork.

7 The threads either side of the centre are worked like this. Add corks to the outer threads.

8 Finish the ends with alternating chains. Thread on corks, as shown here. Trim the ends.

3-D Macramé

1 Mount 12 threads at the top of the ring. Tie two groups of hitches (14, Sampler Two). Repeat inwards.

2 Tie square knots with outer two threads from each group. Mount six threads on ring each side and tie.

3 Tie horizontal hitches as shown. Tie the threads to the ring (4). Bind the ring (5).

You will need:
100g (4oz) natural berber yarn
Oddments of 2-ply rug yarn in scarlet, maroon and cerise pink
Wooden or plastic ring 150mm (6in) in diameter
Softboard and pins
Crochet hook
Darning needle

Length of threads:
24 berber threads 2.25m (2¼yd) long

Macramé is a versatile and flexible craft which lends itself well to the third dimension. This offers many exciting possibilities, and is not as complex as it may seem.

Working three-dimensionally with macramé offers a great deal of scope for invention. You are taking soft and pliable materials and moulding them into pieces of work which are sculptural, and when you embark on a piece of work in this way you may not be sure of how the finished item will look. Do not feel you have to set out with a fixed idea of the finished design in your mind. It is better to be flexible and adapt your patterns and knots as the work takes shape in front of you.

This is part of the enjoyment of macramé.

The project shown here is a small three-dimensional hanging which serves as a good introduction. It is made in berber yarn, which, being a coarse type of weaving yarn, will tie into quite firm knots that are easy to mould into shape. For much more solid knots, which will hold their shape better, you could substitute the kinds of strings and twines which you find in gardening shops. In fact, the stiffer cords are the most suitable for three-dimensional macramé.

4 Use this method to tie the threads to the base of the ring.

5 Bind the top of the ring with maroon yarn as shown.

6 Tie two more groups of diagonal hitches below ring. Continue centre braids of square knots.

7 Pull two groups together with another square knot braid. Wrap the threads and loop up into back.

8 Wrap threads (6, Mounting and Finishing). Darn the ends a little way down with a needle and trim.

9 Detail of the back. The wrapped threads are looped and twined around, then hooked into the back.

The basis of the knots shown here is a ring which can be made of plastic, bamboo, cane or wood (1, 5). The main area of knots is in berber yarn, and consists entirely of horizontal clove hitches, worked diagonally in various directions, and of square knot braids. The brightly coloured coils are the ends of the threads, which are wrapped and looped around one another and then hooked through into the back of the knots. This hanging is a good example of how you can achieve an intricate effect using only two basic knots.

To begin, mount 12 of the berber threads to the top of the ring and pin them down onto your working board. They are then knotted in two groups with five rows of diagonal clove hitches sloping down from the centre. The last thread on each row is left free, so you can tie five more rows inwards close to the first groups. This area is then formed into a curve by taking the outer two threads from each group and tying them in a square knot. Continue with more square knots until you reach the base of the ring (1, 2). The steps on this page show how the additional threads are mounted each side of the ring in two groups of six, then tied in hitches, which meet the central groups. The 10 threads either side of the centre square knot then continue to the base of the ring.

The threads are attached to the ring (4). Keep the knots fairly tight, so that the area inside the ring maintains its shape.

Continue the first square knot braid to the tip of the hanging, and again hold the second curved section of knots in place by another square knot braid (6).

Step 7 shows how the rest of the threads have been wrapped and looped into an attractive pattern.

You can do this as freely as you want, depending on what sort of shape you want your hanging to have. As you twist the wrapped coloured threads into various formations, so you will see the hanging develop its individual character.

Step 9 shows the back of the hanging to illustrate how the ends are hooked through and finished off.

Variations
The hanging shown here is not wholly three-dimensional as it cannot really be looked at from all sides. If you want to make something that is completely free-hanging, a simple way to begin is by working on a ring suspended from its centre with threads mounted all round. To increase the dimension, you can add more threads at various stages by mounting new threads on to existing ones with lark's head knots. Shapes can be turned into forms by looping groups of threads over, through or across others. In the same way, new colours or contrasting weights and textures of yarn or string can be added to give more interest.

Another way of beginning three-dimensional macramé is to mount your threads onto a piece of driftwood, or onto wire which you can bend into an unusual shape, or onto straight metal rods or dowel which you can tie together at angles rather than working down from them in a flat way. Try experimenting with the shapes of the knots by looking at them from all angles — you may find that what started as the top of your work might look more pleasing from another angle, and you could add more threads to work in another direction.

List of Suppliers

Great Britain
Suppliers who operate a mail order system are marked with an asterisk*

Arthur Beale Ltd
194 Shaftesbury Avenue
London WC2

Craftsman's Mark Yarns*
Trefnant
Denbighshire
North Wales

Dryad Ltd*
Northgates
Leicestershire
(mail order only)

Ells and Farrier
The Bead Shop
5 Princes Street
London W1

William Hall & Co (Monsall) Ltd*
177 Stanley Road
Cheadle Hulme
Cheadle
Cheshire

The Handweavers Studio and Gallery*
29 Haroldstone Road
Walthamstow
London E17

Hobby Horse
15–17 Langton Street
London SW10

J. Hyslop Bathgate & Co*
Island Street
Galashiels
Selkirkshire
Scotland

John Lewis
Oxford Street
London W1
(and branches)

Reeves/Dryad Craft Shop
178 Kensington High Street
London W8

The Rope Shop
26 High Street
Emsworth
Hampshire

Texere Yarns*
9 Peckover Street
Bradford
Yorkshire

U.S.A.

U.S. readers are advised to go to their local yarn and weaving equipment suppliers, handicraft stores, or to the notions and fabrics sections of department stores for yarns, fabrics and small pieces of equipment.

Some further reading

Encyclopedia of Needlework
Thérèse de Dillmont,
Dillmont, Mulhouse, France;
Toggitt, New York;
Bailey Bros., U.K.

The Ashley Book of Knots
Clifford Ashley,
Doubleday, New York;
Faber, London

Encyclopedia of Knots and Fancy Rope Work
Raoul Graumont and John Hensel,
Cornell Maritime Press,
Cambridge, Maryland, U.S.A.

Macramé: The Art of Creative Knotting
Virgina Harvey,
Van Nostrand Reinhold, New York

Design & Color in Macramé
Virgina Harvey,
Van Nostrand Reinhold, New York

Knots and Netting
Irene Waller
Studio Vista, London;
Taplinger, New York

Publications

Crafts
Crafts Advisory Committee
28, Haymarket
London SW1

Craft Horizons
American Crafts Council
44 West 53rd Street
New York, N.Y. 10019